Duke has expected—and produced—great results on the court. With Krzyzewski leading the way, there is no question that the expectation to be great will continue.

"I want Duke basketball to be good on a continuing basis," Krzyzewski said. "All along it has been my goal to give Duke a program that will last, one that will be nationally ranked and worthy of postseason play every year."

NEW AGE OF DEVILS

TIMELINE

Wilbur Wade "Cap" Card introduces basketball at Trinity College.

The Blue Devils meet up with North Carolina for the first time on the basketball court. Through 2011, the heated rivals had played each other 232 times.

Trinity College changes its name to Duke University. It is named after the Duke family.

Eddie Cameron begins his first season as Duke's coach. The Blue Devils join the Southern Conference.

Cameron takes over as athletic director and football coach at Duke. With too much on his plate, Cameron resigns as the basketball coach, ending a 14-year tenure. Gerry Gerard replaces him.

1906 1920 1924 1928 1942

Duke makes a change at head coach, as Bradley leaves for Texas. Vic Bubas replaces him.

Led by Bubas, the Blue Devils advance to the NCAA Tournament finals for the first time. They lose to UCLA and finish second.

Bucky Waters is named the head coach of the Blue Devils, replacing Bubas. During the next 11 years, the Blue Devils have three different head coaches.

Just 33 years old, Mike Krzyzewski takes the head coaching job at Duke. He coached Army for five seasons before arriving in Durham.

Duke wins its first national championship. The Blue Devils cap a 32–7 season with a win against Kansas in the championship game.

1959 1964 1969 1980 1991

Coach Gerard resigns after eight seasons, citing poor health. Harold Bradley replaces him. Early in 1951, Gerard passes away from cancer.

Dick Groat is the first Duke player to earn National Player of the Year honors. As of 2011, nine different Blue Devils have received that honor.

For the first time, Duke finishes a season ranked nationally. It finishes 12th.

After 25 seasons in the Southern Conference, Duke is one of seven schools to join forces and create the ACC. The Blue Devils have been in the ACC ever since.

Duke reaches the NCAA Tournament for the first time in its history, losing in the first round.

1950 1952 1952 1953 1955

The Blue Devils win the title for the second season in a row. They finish 34–2, including a 71–51 win over Michigan in the finals. In the quarterfinals, Christian Laettner hits his famous game-winning shot in overtime to defeat Kentucky.

Duke reaches the NCAA Tournament finals but loses to Connecticut. Four Duke players are taken in the first round of the NBA Draft.

Led by two players who received National Player of the Year awards during their careers—Shane Battier and Jason Williams—Duke wins its third national title. The Blue Devils defeat Arizona in the title game.

Duke guard J. J. Redick and forward Sheldon Williams finish their four-year careers at Duke. Redick's 457 three-pointers are an NCAA record while Williams leaves as Duke's career leader in blocked shots and rebounds.

Rolling to a 35–5 record, Duke wins the national championship for the fourth time. It defeats Butler in the championship game.

1992 1999 2001 2006 2010

PROGRAM INFO

Trinity College (1906–24)
Duke University Blue Devils (1924–)

NCAA TOURNAMENT FINALS
(WINS IN BOLD)

1964, 1978, 1986, 1990, **1991**, **1992**, 1994, 1999, **2001**, **2010**

OTHER ACHIEVEMENTS

Final Fours: 15
NCAA Tournaments: 35
ACC Tournament Titles: 19

KEY PLAYERS
(POSITION(S), YEARS WITH TEAM)

Shane Battier (F; 1997–2001)
Elton Brand (F; 1997–99)
Johnny Dawkins (G; 1982–86)
Danny Ferry (F; 1985–89)
Mike Gminski (C; 1976–80)
Dick Groat (G; 1949–52)
Art Heyman (F; 1960–63)
Grant Hill (G/F; 1990–94)
Bobby Hurley (G; 1989–93)
Christian Laettner (C; 1988–92)
Trajan Langdon (G; 1994–99)

Jeff Mullins (F; 1961–64)
J. J. Redick (G; 2002–06)
Bob Verga (G; 1964–67)
Jason Williams (G; 1999–2002)
Shelden Williams (F; 2002–06)
Corren Youmans (F; 1946–50)

KEY COACHES

Vic Bubas (1959–69):
    213–67; 11–4 (NCAA Tournament)
Eddie Cameron (1928–42):
    226–99
Mike Krzyzewski (1980–):
    827–225; 79–23 (NCAA Tournament)

HOME ARENA

Cameron Indoor Stadium (1940–)

* All statistics through 2010–11 season

Duke has a famous and intense rivalry with North Carolina that dates back to 1920. The Blue Devils' rivalry with North Carolina State has actually been in existence longer, however. The two schools first met in basketball on February 9, 1912, with Duke winning 31–28. Through 2011, the teams had faced each other 235 times, with Duke winning 138 of those games.

"Krzyzewskiville" has become a famous part of the culture at Duke. Prior to some home games, students camp out in tents outside of Cameron Indoor Stadium in an effort to get the best seats in the building. Often, more than 1,000 students will camp out before the two designated "tenting" games each season. Some students have been known to camp out for as long as 10 weeks. Prior to coach Mike Krzyzewski's arrival, the area was known as "Tent City." Krzyzewski will talk to students before the tenting games. He also has sent pizzas to them as a gesture of thanks for their loyalty to Duke basketball.

In addition to basketball players, Duke has had some famous students pass through its halls. Among them is Richard Nixon, the thirty-seventh president of the United States, who received a law degree from Duke.

"You have to follow your heart and lead with it and Duke has always taken up my whole heart." —Duke coach Mike Krzyzewski

GLOSSARY

All-American
A group of players chosen as the best amateurs in the country in a particular activity.

assist
A pass that leads directly to a made shot.

athletic director
An administrator who oversees the coaches, players, and teams of an institution.

conference
In sports, a group of teams that plays each other each season.

draft
A system used by professional sports leagues to select new players in order to spread incoming talent among all teams. The NBA Draft is held each June.

overtime
A period in a basketball game that is played to determine a winner when the four quarters end in a tie.

rebound
To secure the basketball after a missed shot.

retire
To officially end one's career. If a team retires a jersey number, no future player is allowed to wear it for that team.

rivalry
When opposing teams bring out great emotion in each team, its fans, and its players.

seed
In basketball, a ranking system used for tournaments. The best teams earn a number one seed.

FURTHER READING

Bowling, Lewis. *Duke Basketball: A Pictorial History*. Charleston, SC: The History Press, 2008.

Krzyzewski, Mike. *Beyond Basketball: Coach K's Keywords for Success*. New York: Warner Books, 2006.

Roth, John. *The Encyclopedia of Duke Basketball*. Durham, NC: Duke University Press, 2006.

WEB LINKS

To learn more about the Duke Blue Devils, visit ABDO Publishing Company online at **www.abdopublishing.com.** Web sites about the Blue Devils are featured on our Book Links page. These links are routinely monitored and updated to provide the most current information available.

PLACES TO VISIT

Cameron Indoor Stadium
115 Whitford Drive
Durham, NC 27708
877-375-DUKE (tickets)
http://www.goduke.com/ViewArticle. dbml?DB_OEM_ID=4200&ATCLID=218099

This is the home arena for the Duke men's and women's basketball teams.

College Basketball Experience
1401 Grand Boulevard
Kansas City, MO 64106
816-949-7500
www.collegebasketballexperience.com

This interactive museum allows visitors to experience various aspects of college basketball. It also includes the National Collegiate Basketball Hall of Fame.

Duke Basketball Museum & Sports Hall of Fame
Durham, NC 27708
919-613-7500
http://www.durham-nc.com/media/ evergreens-backgrounders/education/ duke_hall_of_fame.php

This museum, located next to Cameron Indoor Stadium, highlights the history and tradition of Duke University basketball.

INDEX

ABOUT THE AUTHOR

Brian Howell is a freelance writer based in Denver, Colorado, who has written several books for youth. He has been a sports journalist for more than 18 years, writing about high school, college, and professional athletics, including covering major sporting events such as the US Open golf tournament, the World Series, the Stanley Cup playoffs, and the NBA All-Star Game and playoffs. Howell has earned several writing awards during his career. He lives with his wife and four children in his native Colorado.